A BRIEF HISTORY OF THE GENOCIDE AGAINST THE SYRIAC ARAMEANS

A BRIEF HISTORY OF THE GENOCIDE AGAINST THE SYRIAC ARAMEANS

JOHNNY SHABO

Translated from the Dutch

2018

Author: Johnny Shabo
© Johnny Shabo, 2018
Originally published in Dutch under the title De genocide
op Arameeërs in het kort.
ISBN: 9789082945706

Jesus said to her, "I am the resurrection and the life. The one who believes in me will live, even though they die; and whoever lives by believing in me will never die.

(John 11:25-26 New International Version)

This translation was made possible through the generosity of Mr. Faruk Faal and Mrs. Susan Faal-Takak

Contents

Foreword

In 1915, in what was then known as the Ottoman (Turkish) Empire, an atrocious genocide took place against Arameans, Armenians and other Christian minorities. The massacre was a preconceived plan to completely cleanse present-day Turkey from these indigenous Christian communities. Appalling crimes have taken place in the Ottoman Empire. Innocent men, women and children were slaughtered without mercy. It was the first genocide of the 20th century, and it became a prototype for the genocides that followed. A genocide concerns acts aimed at the destruction of a national, ethnic, racial or religious group (The United Nations, 1948). In recent years, the Armenian genocide has gathered increasing attention. However, the fact that Arameans were also victims of the same genocide, has received considerably less consideration. There are relatively few Dutch-language publications about the genocide against Arameans. This unfortunate gap in historical consciousness prompted me to write this booklet, hopefully providing a clear and insightful picture of the genocide against the Arameans. The crimes that took place in 1915 should never be forgotten, and if we fail to learn from our own dark history, it will continue to repeat itself.

From an early age I heard stories about the mass murders that took place in 1915. Three of my grandparents were children of genocide survivors. My paternal grandfather witnessed the genocide first hand.

He was 10 years old at the time. His full name was Jesjoea Shabo Chawadja. His first and last name give away his Christian background. Jesjoea is the Hebrew-Aramaic name of Jesus, Shabo means 'Saturday' in Aramaic, and Chawadja is an honorary title used for wealthy Christians or Jews (Shwartz, 2005, p. 5). Archpriest Henno records my family as one of the prominent Aramean families at the time of the genocide of 1915 (Henno, 1977/2005, p. 37). On my father's side, the family originally came from Aleppo. They moved to the current Turkish province of Mardin before 1915. At the time, this entire area was occupied by the Ottoman Empire. However, like a large part of the south of present-day Turkey, Mardin was part of historical Syria. Antioch, for example, which is now in Turkey, was the capital of Syria for centuries. The move from Aleppo is therefore comparable to a move within the borders of a contemporary modern state. The 1915 genocide left its marks on the collective memory of my family. It has cost the lives of 12 family members. After the genocide, my grandfather, along with his family, fled to the French mandate established after the First World War, a region that would later witness the emergence of the modern states of Syria and Lebanon. Eventually, my family settled in Damascus, where I was born. After the bloodshed ceased, part of my family tried to make a fresh start in modern-day Turkey, but this was made impossible. Iskandar, my grandfather's cousin and the most prominent member of the family, was beheaded in a horrible way. His eldest son, Afedmeshiho, succeeded him as chawadja, but was shot dead. As of 2018, none of my relatives live in Turkey.

Before describing the genocide, I will give a brief historical introduction concerning the Arameans and the position of Arameans within the Ottoman Empire. After that, I will discuss the developments leading up to the genocide, then describe the genocidal process itself, its consequences and the aftermath of the genocide. I will also briefly describe the positive role that the Yazidis played during the genocide and how some towns and regions developed into safe havens. Finally, I will discuss how history repeats itself in modern-day Syria and Iraq.

Historical introduction

"When you get there, anoint Hazael king over Aram."

(1 Kings 19:15)

Arameans are indigenous people of the Middle East. Starting in the 12th century BC, Arameans began to play an important role in the Middle East. They founded various Aramean kingdoms, such as Bit Bahani, Bit Gabbari, Bit Agusi, Hamat, Matiatu and Aram-Damascus (Brock & Taylor, 2001, pp. 61-73 part 1). The patriarch Abraham himself was an Aramean (Deuteronomy 26:5). Wonderful stories about Arameans are recorded in the Bible, such as the story of Rachel and her beloved Jacob. Jacob fled to the plains of Aram, near present-day Urfa (Turkey). He had to work for a total of 14 years in order to marry Rachel, daughter of Laban the Aramean (Genesis 28-31). Aramean kings are frequently mentioned in the Bible, such as King Hazael, who was the only non-Jewish king to be anointed by a biblical prophet (1 Kings 19:15; O-bible.com). The language of the Arameans dominated the Middle East for centuries. Aramaic became the official language of the Persian Empire. It developed from a trade language into a rich, literary tongue (Brock & Taylor, 2001, p. 14, part 1). Even Jesus spoke Aramaic (MacLeod, 2015, p. 1). Many famous Aramean authors have made significant contributions to global, cultural, scientific and religious developments.

Notable examples are Church Father St. Ephrem, called the crown of all Arameans (Den Biesen, 2014, p. 61) and patriarch Michael the great, author of probably the largest medieval chronicle (archive.org, 2013).

Aramean kingdoms	Modern names	Country
Aram-Damascus	Damascus	Syria
Bit Bahani	Tell Halaf, on the river Khabur	Syria
Bit Agusi	Arpad (Aleppo province)	Syria
Hamat	Hama	Syria
Bit Gabbari	Zencirli (Gazintep)	Turkey
Bit Zamani	Diyarbakir	Turkey
Matiatu	The eastern part of Mardin province (Tur Abdin)	Turkey

(Brock & Taylor, 2001, pp. 61-73 part 1)

Arameans converted to Christianity in the first centuries AD. Cities such as Antioch (Antakya), Edessa (Urfa), Nisibin (Nusaybin), Melitene (Malatya), Tikrit, Reshaino (Ras al-Ayn), Qenneshre (Qinnasrin), Mabbug (Manbij), Apamia, Sadad and Damascus became important Christian centers. From dozens of monasteries such as the Monastery of Qenneshre, the St. Ananias Monastery (Mardin) and the St. Moses Monastery (An-Nabek), monks produced countless numbers of books and writings related to theology, philosophy, astronomy and history (Brock & Taylor, 2001, pp. 27-166 part 2).

16

Various churches have arisen that use or have used Syriac-Aramaic as a church language in the past. The Greek Orthodox Church of Antioch and the Greek-Catholic Church of Antioch have not used Aramaic as a church language since the 17th century. The other churches shown in the diagram below still use Syriac-Aramaic, either as their principal church language, or as one of the church languages.

Churches that use Syriac-Aramaic as church language or have used it in the past

Churches	Other names	Denominations	Historical seat of the patriarch
Syriac Orthodox Church	Jacobites	Oriental orthodox	Antioch
Syriac Catholic Church	Uniate Church	Catholic	Antioch
Syriac Maronite Church	Maronites	Catholic	Antioch
Greek Orthodox Church of Antioch	Rum or Melkites	Eastern orthodox	Antioch
Melkite Greek Catholic Church	Rum or Melkites	Catholic	Antioch
Church of the East	Nestorians or Assyrians	Nestorian	Ctesiphon (Madain)
Chaldean Catholic Church	Chaldeans	Catholic	Ctesiphon (Madain)

(Brock & Taylor, 2001, pp. 11-64 part 3; Courtois, 2004, p. 228).

Note for the reader

From the fifth century onwards, the Arameans adopted the Greek term Syrians (Suryoye) when referring to themselves. The terms Syrians and Arameans were used as synonyms (Iwas, 1983). The NBG 1951 (Dutch) Bible translation speaks of Arameans, the Statenvertaling (Dutch) Bible translation of Syrians. Confusion began after the establishment of the modern Arab state of Syria (1946). Until the founding of the modern state of Syria, the term Syrians was only intended to designate the indigenous Aramean population of Syria, Iraq and southern Turkey. The Dutch word "Syrisch" thus relates to two different population groups: the Aramean Christians on the one hand, and all the inhabitants of Syria on the other (Leijsen, 2015). In order to avoid confusion with the predominantly Arab inhabitants of Syria, this book speaks only of Arameans. As far as the sources are concerned, this book considers the terms Arameans and Syrians/Syriacs[1] as identical as long as it relates to Aramean Christians.

---

[1] For some decades, the English term Syriac has been used to distinguish Aramean Christians from the current predominantly Arab inhabitants of Syria, but because the term Syriac is very similar to Syrian, it continues to cause confusion.

Under the yoke of the sick man of Europe

For the past two millennia, Arameans have enjoyed little or no political power. Until the 7th century, the Romans dominated the political arena in the Middle East. From the 7th century onwards, various Islamic empires were in control. The last major Islamic power was the Ottoman (Turkish) Empire. The Ottoman Empire, also known as the Caliphate, has for centuries dominated the Middle East, as well as large parts of North Africa and Eastern Europe. Of great symbolic importance was the Ottoman conquest of Constantinople in 1453. Constantinople was the capital of the Eastern Roman (Byzantine) Empire for a period of over 1000 years, representing a continuity of Roman civilization. Also, the patriarch of some 300 million Eastern Orthodox Christians still resides in Constantinople, present-day Istanbul.

Before the genocide of 1915, practically all Arameans lived in the Ottoman Empire, mainly in the southeast of present-day Turkey. Arameans inhabited cities such as Beth Zabday (Azech/Idil), Omid (Diyarbakir), Urhoi (Urfa), Nisibin (Nusaybin), Adiyaman, Adana and Mardin, which means 'fortresses' in Aramaic (Armalet, 1919, p. 1). They also lived in the Besheriye plain, in the vicinity of the town of Omid (Diyarbakir) and in the Tur Abdin region, which means 'mountain of the servants (of God)' in Aramaic. Tur Abdin corresponds roughly to the eastern part of the current Mardin province.

Arameans have been living in this region since the ninth century BC (Brock & Taylor, 2001, p. 62, part 1). In addition to Southeast Turkey, Arameans mainly lived in Syrian places such as Sadad, Zaidal, Fairuze, Homs, Al-Qaryatayn, Maaloula, Damascus and Aleppo.

General habitat of the Arameans in 1914

Apart from the Arameans, the south-east of present-day Turkey was mainly populated by Kurds. Leaders of Kurdish tribes dominated this area. At the beginning of the 20th century, Kurdish tribal leaders enjoyed great freedom. Ottoman rulers pretty much allowed them to do whatever they wanted (Courtois, 2004, p. 53). The position of Arameans worsened as a result.

Leaders of Kurdish tribes addressed Christians with the Kurdish words Felhe me, which means 'my Christian' in Kurdish. Christians had to answer with the Kurdish words es goelam, which means 'your servant' (Holslag, 2010, p. 109). This clearly shows how the relationships were before the genocide took place. Arameans were oppressed by Kurdish tribal leaders.

The position of Arameans within the Ottoman Empire was largely determined by their Christian faith. For centuries, the Arameans, like other Christian inhabitants of the Ottoman Empire, had become accustomed to the dhimmi status. The designate dhimmi is used for a Jew or Christian who has acknowledged the superiority of Islam and lives under Islamic supreme authority (Jansen, 2008, p. 123). All Christian minorities within the Ottoman Empire had to pay a special tax. In addition, they had to deal with all kinds of discriminatory laws (Zwaan, 2001, p. 218). For example, they were not allowed to ride a horse and their houses had to be lower than those of their Muslim neighbors. In the case of legal disputes, Christians were not allowed to testify against Muslims (Jenkins, 2011, p. 221). In many ways it was made clear that they, as Christians, were considered inferior to Muslims. For example, Christians had to pay a special tax and had fewer rights. The collection of the special tax was anchored in the so-called millet system. A millet was an officially recognized religious community within the Ottoman Empire. Every non-Islamic community formed its own millet. Although the term millet originally means 'nation' (derived from the Arabic word milla), it has little to do with an ethnic nation.

For example, Syriac Catholics and Chaldean Catholic Christians fell under the Armenian-Catholic millet, although each have a different ethnic background. Religious affiliation was of decisive importance. Arameans belonged to the Syriac Orthodox, Armenian Catholic and Protestant millet. A millet was used by the Ottoman authorities to collect the special tax for non-Muslims through the structure of the religious institutions. Before the genocide, six non-Muslim religious communities were officially recognized within the Ottoman Empire.

Non-Islamic religious communities recognized within the Ottoman Empire (1915)

- Greek Orthodox millet
- Armenian Orthodox millet
- Armenian Catholic millet
- Syriac Orthodox millet
- Protestant millet
- Jewish millet

(Hofmann, 2005, p. 141 & 142; D'Avril, 2013, p. 86)

At the time of the Ottoman Empire, Arameans, like other Christians, had to deal with persecutions on a regular basis. In 1860, thousands of Maronite Christians were murdered in Lebanon. This outburst of violence spread to cities like Damascus, where the Christian part of the city was plundered. Thousands of Christian residents of Damascus were slaughtered (The New York Times, 1860).

Dozens of churches were set on fire. In 1895 and 1896, Aramean Christians were the victims of pogroms carried out by Hamidiye corps, paramilitary forces consisting mainly of Kurdish fighters who operated on behalf of the Turkish sultan. The inhabitants of Urhoi (Urfa), Omid (Diyarbakir), Qarabash, Qatarbel, Sadiye, Mipharaqat, Adiyaman, Frobat (Elazig), Benebil and the Besheriye plain were the victims of violent attacks. At least 25 thousand innocent Arameans were murdered in 1895 and 1896 (Brock & Taylor, 2001, p. 66 part 3). Arameans, like other Christian minorities, were regularly subjected to slaughter by order of or with the approval of the Ottoman rulers.

An incomplete list of pogroms against Christians in the Ottoman Empire

Year	Location	Number of dead
1850	The Aleppo massacre (Masters, 1990, pp. 3-20)	Unknown
1860	Pogrom of Damascus (The New York Times, 1860)	8.000
1892	Lootings in Mardin (Courtois, 2004, p. 102)	Unknown
1895	Hamidian massacres near Diyarbakir (Courtois, 2004, p. 112)	30.000
1896	Hamidian massacres in Urfa (Awad & Obeid, 2015, p. 15)	13.000
1909	The Adana massacre (Armstrong, 2016)	30.000

The Christian quarter of Damascus after the 1860 pogrom.

On the eve of the genocide

The Ottoman (Turkish) Empire dominated the Middle East and the Balkans for centuries. Serbia, Greece, Bulgaria, Hungary, Romania, Montenegro, Egypt, Tunisia, Libya, Algeria, Syria, Iraq, Jordan, Lebanon and Turkey were under Ottoman rule. The Ottoman Empire even threatened Western Europe, but after the failed siege of Vienna in 1683, the power of the Ottoman Empire began to wane. The emerging European nations gained more and more ground. European countries such as the Netherlands, Spain and Portugal already dominated world trade in the 17th century. By using the sea route to Asia, these emerging powers circumvented the ancient silk route that ran through the Ottoman Empire. At the time of the Enlightenment in the 18th century, the control of European powers increased even further. Due to modernization and the strong development of European countries in the fields of jurisprudence, literature, science and culture, the position of the Ottoman Empire deteriorated compared to European countries. This ultimately resulted not only in the stagnation of Ottoman expansion, but also in various wars of independence in the 19th century, which in turn resulted in the independence of Greece, Serbia, Bulgaria, Montenegro and Romania, among others. The Ottoman Empire lost territory in the 18th and 19th centuries and the economic and political system of the Ottoman Empire came under pressure. The old economic system of the Empire was based on territorial expansion. By conquering new areas, the conquered peoples could be subjected and exploited.

For example, the elite troops (the janissaries) of the Ottoman army were made up of children of Christians who were enslaved. Young boys were taken away from their homes and brought up as Muslim men. They were then trained to become professional soldiers who played a very important role within the Ottoman army (Hain, 2012, p. 1). Due to the immense loss of territory, the economy of the Ottoman Empire stagnated, the very core of which was based on territorial expansion. The Ottoman Empire was called the sick man of Europe. Prior to the genocide of 1915, the process of stagnation and decline accelerated. In 1912, the Balkan wars broke out. Greece, which was only too happy to liberate the large Greek population still living under Ottoman rule, fought alongside Serbia, Bulgaria and Montenegro against the Ottoman Empire. The results of the Balkan wars were disastrous for the Ottoman Empire. Almost all remaining European territory was lost. The capital (Istanbul) was almost occupied. In addition, the Balkan wars had major demographic consequences. For the first time in the history of the Ottoman Empire, Muslims formed the majority. Although the power lay with the Islamic elite, until 1913 the majority of the population was Christian. Due to the loss of many territories in the 19th century and the loss of almost all remaining European territories in 1913, for the first time in its recorded history, Christians no longer held the majority in the Ottoman Empire.

The series of defeats against Christian countries such as Greece, Bulgaria and Serbia strengthened nationalism. Many Turkish intellectuals and military sought refuge in emerging nationalism.

This eventually led to a bloody coup. In 1913, the young Turks of the Committee for Unity and Progress seized power through a coup d'état. Formally, the sultan remained in power, but the real power lay with Talaat, Enver and Djemal, the three prominent leaders of the Committee for Unity and Progress. Talaat became the Minister of the Interior. Enver became the Minister of War, and Djemal became the Minister of the Navy. The Committee for Unity and Progress was initially fed by three movements: Ottomanism, Islamism and Turkism (Ungor, 2012, p. 47). Partly due to the loss of territory, the ideology of the Committee for Unity and Progress continued to radicalize, and the emphasis was mainly on the Turkification of the Ottoman Empire. Perhaps Turkish intellectuals attributed the modernization of European countries to the fact that they were nation states.

Timeline of territorial losses of the Ottoman Empire

1878   Recognition of the independence of Serbia

1881   France conquers Algeria

1908   Independence of Bulgaria

1913   Loss of almost all European territories

Although the ties between the regime and Christian subjects like Arameans were particularly bad, the aversion of the new elite against Armenians and other Christian minorities continued to increase. The new regime of the young Turks became a radical nationalistic dictatorship that increasingly inclined towards the establishment of the Ottoman Empire as a homogeneous Turkish state.

In this homogeneous state there was no place for Christian minorities who were regarded as outsiders, even though the Christian subjects had been living in present-day Turkey for thousands of years, as in the case of the Armenians and the Arameans. Remarkably, the anger of the new regime was not aimed at non-Turkish Muslim minorities such as the Kurds, despite the fact that the new policy was aimed at the Turkification of the Ottoman Empire.

The Armenian and Greek populations formed the largest Christian minorities. The Armenians experienced a true renaissance at the end of the 19th century. An Armenian elite arose that played a prominent economic role. Armenian importers, exporters, industrialists and craftsmen dominated the economy of the Ottoman Empire. Armenians founded Armenian schools, hospitals and institutions. This led to envy among Muslim compatriots. In addition, the Armenian minority was increasingly seen as a threat by the young Turks' regime. Aramean Christians comprised a small minority, concentrated in the southeast of Turkey. Until 1915, Arameans had never openly opposed the Ottoman rulers in any significant way. They remained loyal despite the oppression and the outright persecution that wasn't seldom their fate. Until 1915, not a single incident was reported in which Arameans protested or used violence against the Ottoman sovereigns. Also, Arameans had never shown national aspirations. In spite of this, Arameans, like other Christian minorities, became victims of the genocide that took place in 1915.

The genocide

"In 1915 the Turkish Government began and ruthlessly carried out the infamous general massacre."

Sir Winston Churchill

(Churchill, 1929)

On July 28, 1914 the First World War broke out and on November 11 of the same year the Ottoman Empire joined Germany and Austria-Hungary in the fight against the Allied forces led by Russia, France and the United Kingdom. Three days later a big manifestation was organized in Istanbul. In front of a large crowd, the highest Islamic clergyman of the Ottoman Empire read out loud a decree calling for the defense of the Ottoman Empire (Zürcher, 2016, p. 20). The army was mobilized. All young men, including Arameans, had to serve in the army. In the collective memory of Arameans, the mobilization process of the army is known as the seferbelik, which means 'total mobilization' (Kevorkian, 2011, p. 430). Genocide researchers believe that it was around this time, in late 1914 or early 1915, that the decision was taken by the leaders of the Ottoman Empire Talaat, Enver and Djemal to commit the genocide (Zwaan, 2004, p. 2). Already during the mobilization process, it became abundantly clear to the Christian minorities, that a disaster was about to take place. Young Aramean men who were forced to enlist said their goodbyes to their families, as if they knew they would be killed. Soon the Aramean fears became reality.

From February 1915, Christian soldiers, including Arameans, were disarmed and transported to labor battalions. They had to do hard labor such as building roads and fortifications. They were starved, abused or executed. An Aramean soldier named Afedmeshiho ('Christ's servant' in Aramaic) disclosed how Christian soldiers were beaten with sticks until their clothes were soaked with blood. Most Christian soldiers did not survive these labor battalions. They died of hunger or outright murder, carried out by Turkish and Kurdish soldiers. The labor battalions represented the first phase of the genocidal process (Van Qarabash, 1918/2002, pp. 62-70, Zwaan, 2004, p. 5). At the same time, many Aramean men were executed for alleged desertion. On February 18, 1915, twelve Arameans from Qarabash were wrongly accused and sentenced to death. They were executed in various cities inhabited by Arameans, such as Mardin, Urhoi (Urfa) and Omid (Diyarbakir). This caused increasing fear among Arameans, fear for what was to come (Van Qarabash, 1918/2002, p. 60). Incidentally, on 21 February of the same year, a law was passed that offered Christians the opportunity to buy themselves out of enlistment, but for most Aramean men it was already too late. In any case, the sum was too high for most Arameans (Courtois, 2004, p. 154). As thousands of young men had been deported, the Aramean community was already severely weakened.

Following the massacres through labor battalions, the Turkish authorities took measures to prepare the genocide. It began with replacing high-ranking public officials unsympathetic to the destruction of Christian subjects by radical anti-Christian administrators.

For example, the public officials of Omid (Diyarbakir) and Mardin were replaced because of their friendly attitude towards Arameans and Armenians. For the Arameans, the replacement of the governor of Omid (Diyarbakir) by Mehmed Reshid had enormous consequences (Armalet, 1919, p. 149). Most Arameans lived in the province of Diyarbakir, which in 1915 included the towns of Beth Zabday (Idil), Nisibin (Nusaybin) and Mardin. Mehmed Reshid was a Cherkess from the Caucasus region (Hofmann, 2005, p. 152). He was a physician and a fanatical member of the Committee for Unity and Progress. He initiated a special militia led by Aziz Feyzi (Ungor, 2009, pp. 3 & 9) who, together with his cousin Bekir Sidki, played a prominent role in the elimination of the Aramean and Armenian elite in Omid (Diyarbakir). At the same time, a special organization was called into being to carry out the genocide. The Ottoman authorities formed special units (teskilat mahsusa) consisting of 50 armed men (Ungor, 2013). These special units, also known as The Special Organization, have committed the genocide against Arameans in the vicinity of the town of Diyarbakir. They were also involved in the genocide of Arameans in the Nisibin area (Van Qarabash, 1918/2002, pp. 81-96 & 125). A disproportionate number of Kurds and Cherkess were members of these special units (Hofmann, 2005, p. 145).

Concurrent with the formation of these special units, talks were held between government officials and local tribal leaders to prepare for the genocide of Arameans (Armalet, 1919, p. 150). Leaders of Kurdish tribes played a prominent role in the extermination of Arameans.

With both the Armenians and the Arameans, the genocide was carried out by Turks, Kurds and Cherkess, a people from the Caucasus region, but with the Arameans, the massacres were mostly carried out by Kurds. The names of the Kurdish tribal leaders who participated in the genocide are listed in the book of archpriest Sleman Henno (Henno, 1977/2005, pp. 58 & 72).

The first Aramean victims of the genocide belonged to the elite. For that matter, the genocide against the Arameans was a carbon copy of the genocide against the Armenians. The elite was pre-selected and slain. 24 April is known as the date on which the Armenian elite was arrested (Zwaan, 2004, p. 5). Less well-known is the fact that Aramean leaders were also arrested and murdered. For example, 1200 Aramean and Armenian notables were arrested in Diyarbakir between 10 and 30 May (Lepsius, 1919, p. 75). They were killed outside the town. It was clear that the governor of Diyarbakir Mehmed Reshid did not distinguish between Armenians and Arameans. In Mardin too, the notables were initially arrested and later murdered (Ungor, 2009, pp. 4, 5 & 9). In Midyat, the Aramean mayor was arrested and murdered. Later, another prominent Aramean leader from Midyat was beheaded who had previously received a medal from Sultan Abdul Hamid (Gaunt, 2006, pp. 188-196).

After the Aramean elite had been eliminated, the mass murder of Arameans began. Everywhere in Southeast Turkey, Arameans were the victims of organized military operations with the goal of ending their presence in Turkey once and for all.

Even before the mass murders started, Arameans were disarmed. Houses of Arameans were searched for weapons to avoid possible resistance during the slaughter. This method was applied in all regions, as various sources reported the disarmament of Arameans in, among others, Qarabash, Kabiye, Mardin and Midyat (Van Qarabash, 1918/2002, pp. 81 & 86; Armalet, 1919, p. 140, Henno, 1977/2005, p. 71). It is, incidentally, a proven method: prior to the Hamidian massacres in 1895 and 1896, Christians were also disarmed.

In the vicinity of Diyarbakir, the mass murders already started in April. In Mardin and the Tur Abdin region, the mass murders didn't start until June, but what is particularly striking is how fast it all went. Hundreds of villages and towns were completely cleared from Christians within a few weeks. In the towns, Arameans were arrested in large numbers. Under the guidance of soldiers, they were then killed outside the town. In Mardin, the first convoy of death was formed on 10 June 1915. 417 people were led through the town by soldiers. They were spat on along the way and mocked by the Muslim residents of Mardin. They were then killed at a citadel near Mardin (Armalet, 1919, pp. 184, 185 & 193). In order to facilitate the mass arrests, the homes of Christians in Mardin were marked by means of red crosses (Courtois, 2004, p. 114). Convoys were also formed in Omid (Diyarbakir). Soldiers always formed convoys of about 500 people. They were then murdered just outside the town (Van Qarabash, 1918/2002, p. 64). Smaller places and villages were surrounded by Kurdish paramilitaries or the special units (teskilat mahsusa).

These special units, consisting of 50 armed men, were formed by the Turkish authorities to carry out the genocide (Ungor, 2013). Dozens of Aramean villages such as Qarabash, Kabiye, Qatarbel and Sadiye were attacked by these special units. First the men were killed. Then the women and children were murdered. Women were often sexually abused before being murdered (Ungor, 2017, pp. 39-40).

In the Tur Abdin region, Kurdish tribes fully participated in the killings. Kurdish tribes were armed by the authorities. Under the guidance of the traditional tribal leaders, together with the special units and supported by regular troops, they committed the genocide in the Tur Abdin region. The killings were aimed at both women and men. Sometimes an exception was made for individual women. Young, beautiful women were carefully selected and taken as concubines or sex slaves (Hofmann, 2005, p. 146). In addition, Arameans who wanted to convert to Islam were spared. However, this option was rarely used. Arameans did not want to convert, even if they had to pay for it with their lives (Henno, 1977/2005, pp. 40 & 49).

Occasionally a distinction was made between the different Christian denominations. In Mardin for example, only the Catholic leaders were arrested initially (Armalet, 1919, p. 167). Shortly afterwards, however, orthodox notables were arrested and murdered as well. In the historic town of Nisibin, it was also the Catholic and Protestant Christians who were murdered first, after which the orthodox Christians were slain (Henno, 1977/2005, pp. 42 & 43).

Perhaps it was a conscious policy to reduce possible opposition. Noteworthy is the Armenian Catholic community of Mardin. Although they were members of the Armenian Catholic Church, in the case of Mardin it involved ethnic Arameans. Aramean residents of Mardin who wanted to join the Catholic Church in the 18th century, became members of the Armenian Catholic Church. In the 18th century, there were no Syriac Catholic priests in Mardin, so that Arameans who wanted to join the Catholic Church became members of the Armenian Catholic Church (Courtois, 2004, p. 171).

After the killings stopped, one of the biggest robberies in history started. The Ottoman regime had established Commissions for Abandoned Property that arranged for the confiscation of the property of Christians. This involved both real estate and movable property. Housings, land, gold and silver were seized. The idea was that these possessions would be divided among the local Muslim population and Muslims from the Balkans or the Caucasus. In the redistribution of housing and real estate, the Directorate for the Settlement of Tribes and Immigrants, the Skan Akar Ve Muhacirin Muduriyeti, played an important role (Ungor, 2012, p. 53). Immigrants meant Muslim immigrants from the Balkans or the Caucasus. For example, the Directorate for the Settlement of Tribes and Immigrants reported to the Ministry of the Interior via a telegram that there were deserted villages around Mardin and Midyat and that the immigrants of the cavalry division could settle there.

In the towns of Mardin and Omid (Diyarbakir) alone, 7.5 million Turkish lira worth of gold, precious stones, carpet and antiques was robbed (Hofmann, 2005, pp. 154-155). Various sources describe meticulously how the loot was distributed or sold to the Muslim inhabitants of Southeast Turkey (Van Qarabash, 1918/2002, pp. 130-131). Turkish and Kurdish leaders who had committed genocide through direct involvement in the massive extermination of Arameans, were generously rewarded by the regime. Among other things, Aziz Feyzi obtained the entire Aramean village of Qarabash as a reward for his active role as leader of a special militia involved in the execution of the genocide (Ungor, 2013).

Estimates of the number of deaths as a result of the genocide vary greatly. Due to the lack of reliable demographic data, it is difficult to determine the exact number of fatalities. In addition, these statistics were mainly recorded by clerics. As a result, the number of deaths per Christian denomination was estimated. The Catholic priest Jacques Rhetoré, who witnessed the genocide, spoke about a reduction in the number of Jacobites from 200 thousand to about 60 or 70 thousand in the entire Ottoman Empire. In addition, he mentioned the number of some 14,000 Catholic victims in the province of Diyarbakir (Courtois, 2004, pp. 194 & 195). Taking into account several thousands of Protestant victims, this would mean that about 150,000 Arameans were murdered as a result of the genocide carried out on behalf of the Ottoman regime. Various Aramean sources, however, cite the number of 500,000 deaths (Messo, 2011, p. 725).

On the basis of analyzes by Sebastien de Courtois, one can in any case conclude that 70% of Arameans living in the southeast of Turkey were murdered during the 1915 genocidal process (Courtois, 2004, p. 198). Sebastien de Courtois is the author of The Forgotten Genocide: Eastern Christians, The Last Arameans. This book is perhaps the sole academic treatise that only relates to the genocide of Arameans. Professor Tessa Hofmann, attached to the Free University of Berlin, also estimated the percentage of fatalities to be 70% (Busstra & Postema, 2015). For comparison, approximately 73% of Dutch Jews were murdered as a result of the Holocaust (Holocaust Names Memorial). If the Aramean victims of the mass murders of 1895 and 1917 are taken into account, then the percentage of Arameans killed is much higher than 70%. In 1895, tens of thousands of Arameans were killed by order of the Turkish sultan (Brock & Taylor, 2001, p. 66, part 3). In 1917, the genocide of 1915 was repeated on a smaller scale in parts of the Ottoman Empire, including in the Tur Abdin region (Courtois, 2004, p. 184).

Syriac Catholic bishop Flavianus Michael Malke was one of the victims of the genocide. In 2015 he was beatified by the pope. This photo has been published with permission from His Beatitude Ignatius Youssef III Younan, patriarch of the Syriac Catholic Church of Antioch.

Timeline of the genocide against Arameans (1915)

February 18   Execution of 12 draftees, followed by the labor battalions and the mass murder of draftees (Van Qarabash, 1918/2002, pp. 60-70, Zwaan, 2004, p. 5).

March 25   Mehmed Reshid becomes governor of Omid/Diyarbakir (Ungor, 2009, p. 3).

May 30   Murder of 674 notables from Diyarbakir (Lepsius, 1919, p. 75).

June 10   The first convoy of death departs from Mardin (Armalet, 1919, pp. 184-193).

June 15   Mass murder in the historic town of Nisibin (Henno, 1977/2005, p. 43).

October 30   Telegram to the Ministry of the Interior to house Muslim immigrants from the Balkans in deserted villages around Mardin (Hofmann, 2005, p. 155). It symbolizes the confiscations of possessions that took place after the genocide.

The Yazidis

With every genocide, and in every war, there are people who stand out because of their good and just deeds. This was also the case at the time of the 1915 genocide. The Yazidis in particular stood out during the genocide, because of their courageous behavior. The Yazidis form a small religious minority that mainly lives around the Sinjar Mountains, not far from the current Turkish-Iraqi border. In 1915 and the years that followed, the Yazidis saved the lives of thousands of Aramean and Armenian Christians by taking them in as refugees in the Sinjar Mountains, the home of Yazidis. Thousands of Aramean and Armenian Christians from Southeast Turkey fled to the Sinjar Mountains where they were hospitably received by the Yazidis. On various occasions, the Yazidis even fought against Ottoman troops to protect the lives of displaced Aramean and Armenian Christians (Armalet, 1919, pp. 372-383). Many Christians who had escaped to the Sinjar Mountains eventually settled in other areas, but some remained around the Sinjar Mountains, especially in the town of Sinjar. In 2014, however, Islamic State abruptly ended the presence of the small Christian community in Sinjar. It is painful to see how descendants of genocide survivors had to flee again, just because of their background. In 2014, the Yazidis themselves also became victims of horrendous persecutions by Islamic State.

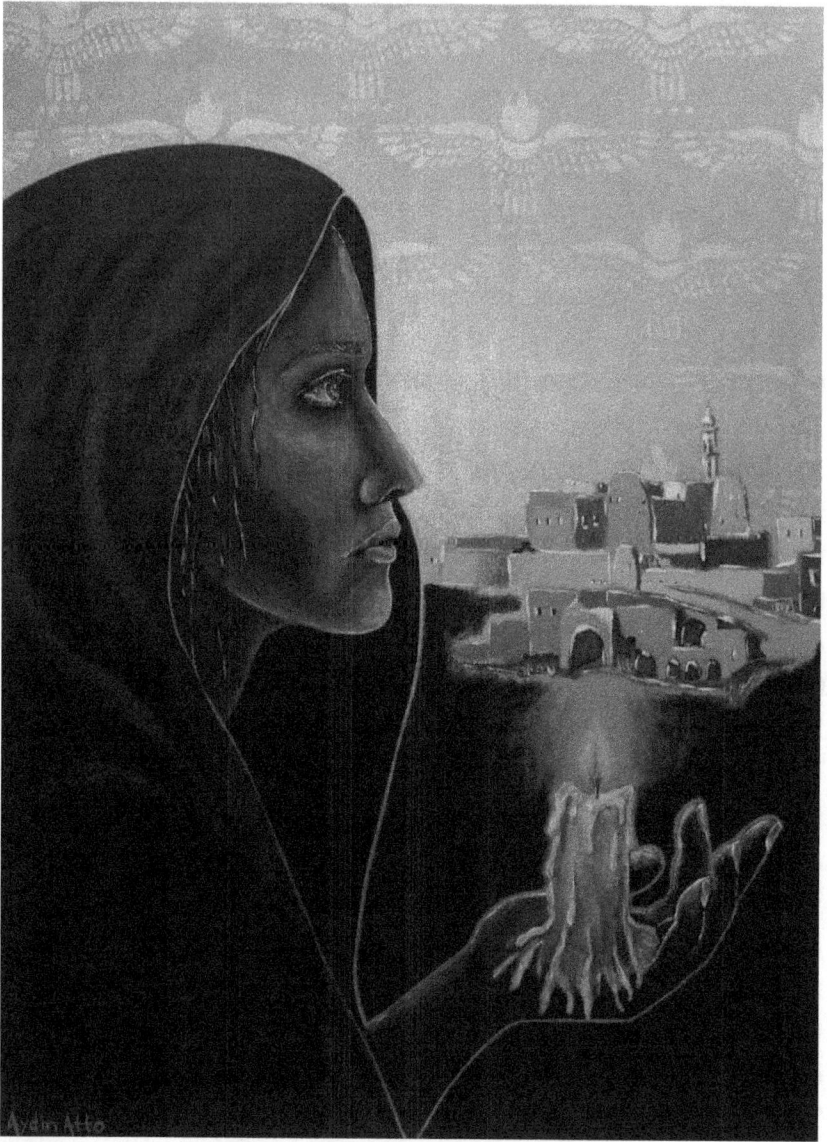

Iwardo, one of the few safe havens at the time of the genocide, painted by Aydin Atto.

HEROIC RESISTANCE

"Even though I walk through the darkest valley, I will fear no evil, for you are with me;"

(Psalm 23:4)

In 1915, in some places like Beth Zabday, Arameans succeeded in successfully defending themselves against repeated attacks by Ottoman troops and Kurdish tribes. Beth Zabday, which means 'house of the gift' in Aramaic, is a historic town. The current Turkish name of this town is Idil. Arameans succeeded in making Beth Zabday an impenetrable fortress. Repeated attacks by Ottoman troops and Kurdish tribes were held off time after time. Beth Zabday was surrounded for months. During the surrounding of Beth Zabday, Ottoman troops led by Omer Naji received support from Kurdish tribes. The attacks took place under the watchful eye of German officers. Germany was an ally of the Ottoman Empire during the genocide (Courtois, 2004, p. 191). Over time, special units (teskilat mahsusa) were sent from Mosul to Beth Zabday. Even Enver, one of the three leaders of the Ottoman regime, personally interfered with the siege of Beth Zabday. For one thing, he sent a telegram to the commander of the third army in Erzurum regarding the attack on Beth Zabday. Enver explains in the telegram that a division led by Naji, along with a battalion of infantry, was en route from Urfa to Jezire to suppress the "rebels" (Enver, 1915). Jezire is near Beth Zabday and there is no doubt that Enver referred to Beth Zabday.

In addition to Beth Zabday, Iwardo developed into a kind of safe haven. Thousands of residents of the surrounding villages became entrenched in the village. The residents of Iwardo, together with thousands of refugees from the area, formed an excellent defense. For months, Iwardo was surrounded by mainly Kurdish fighters. The army that surrounded Iwardo counted some 13,000 fighters, yet ultimately failed to take Iwardo. The thousands of refugees who sought refuge in Iwardo survived the genocide (Armalet, 1919, pp. 405-408). In 2018, Iwardo, meaning 'source of the rose' in Aramaic, is almost exclusively occupied by Kurds.

The aftermath of the genocide

"But even if you should suffer for what is right, you are blessed. "Do not fear their threats; do not be frightened."

(1 Peter 3:14)

The genocide of 1915 almost led to the total destruction of the Aramean civilization. The majority of Arameans was killed. More than 160 churches and monasteries were destroyed (Courtois, 2004, p. 240). Historical libraries containing invaluable books and manuscripts were confiscated, as in the case of the library of St. John's Church in Mardin. Centuries-old centers of Christianity were destroyed in the aftermath of the genocide, such as the St. Gabriel Monastery (Van Qarabash, 1918/2002, p. 122).

Thousands of genocide survivors who fled to other regions were often unable to keep their Aramaic mother tongue alive. Teachers were imprisoned if they taught the Aramaic language (World Council of Arameans, 2015, p. 5). Some Aramaic languages became dead languages because nearly all speakers were murdered, as in the case of Mlahso Aramaic (Messo, 2017, p. 30). Essentially, an end was made of the presence of Arameans in large parts of Turkey. A large proportion of the survivors of the genocide fled the Ottoman Empire. They sought a safe haven in both the Middle East and beyond. Many Arameans emigrated to Brazil, the United States or other Western countries.

Others sought the safety of the French and British mandate areas established in the Middle East after the First World War. Arameans settled in cities like Damascus, Aleppo, Qamishli, Al-Hasakah, Mosul, Sinjar, Beirut, Jerusalem and Bethlehem. A small community remained in the southeast of Turkey. Meanwhile, the regime of young Turks fell in 1918. The sultan seized power and a special tribunal was set up to bring the perpetrators of the genocide to justice for deportation and murder. In 1919, the leaders of the Committee for Unity and Progress were sentenced to death, but in the meantime they had almost all fled abroad (Ungor, 2012, p. 62). Less than a year later, the special tribunal was lifted under pressure from the new rulers operating from Ankara. In 1923, the modern Turkish state was established under the leadership of Atatürk. The new regime soon began to deny the genocide. This denial policy is maintained by the Turkish state to this day. Turkey is even putting countries under pressure not to recognize the genocide. The Turkish government still reacts furiously when a country recognizes the genocide. This became clear in recent decades after many Western parliaments and governments formally acknowledged the genocide (Sommer B., 2018). 28 countries have since recognized the Armenian genocide in which a number of countries, including the Netherlands, explicitly recognized the Arameans as victims of the same genocide (Dutch House of Representatives, 2018).

Even after the genocide of 1915, the oppression of Aramean Christians continued in Turkey. In 1923, the treaty of Lausanne was signed between Turkey and the European countries.

The boundaries of the current Turkish state were determined. In addition, the right of non-Muslim minorities to establish their own churches, schools and institutions in Turkey was guaranteed through this treaty (Treaty of Lausanne - Art: 40). However, the Turkish state applies these rights only to the Armenian, Greek and Jewish minorities, even though no non-Muslim minority is explicitly mentioned in the Lausanne Convention. In practice, the rights of these minorities are also grossly violated, but the fact that Turkey interprets the Lausanne Convention in such a way that it does not apply to Arameans, does have far-reaching consequences. For example, Arameans do not have their own schools, newspapers or magazines in Turkey, as opposed to the Armenians (Sommer R., 2012, p. 163).

However, it was not only the lack of recognition by the Turkish state. Church leaders, such as the Syriac Orthodox patriarch Ignatius Elias, were exiled from Turkey (Luke, 1925, p. 113). For almost 800 years, the patriarch resided in Mardin, and in 1924 this came to an end. The Syriac Catholic patriarch too moved from Mardin to Lebanon after the genocide. Names of villages and towns were changed into Turkish names so that every trace of the Aramean civilization would be wiped out. A policy that was formalized in the 1950s by the establishment of the Special Commission for Name Change, that altered the names of some 12,000 villages and towns into Turkish names by order of the Turkish Ministry of the Interior (Oktem, 2004, p. 569). This policy of Turkification was applied everywhere. This is also the case in the historic town of Urhoi (Urfa), also known as Edessa.

49

Until 1915 there lived a large Aramean community of architects, artisans and traders in Urhoi, but the churches were gradually converted into mosques. Urhoi's Aramaic-language school was confiscated and renamed the Onbir Nissan primary school, a public Turkish school that is still known in Urhoi (Oktem, 2004, p. 571). Traces of Aramean architecture are, however, still visible everywhere in Urhoi.

In the seventies and eighties of the twentieth century, the remaining Aramean community found itself wedged in between the Kurdish PKK and the Turkish army. A large part of the remaining Arameans were forced to flee to Europe, causing the community in Southeast Turkey to become even smaller. In the nineties of the twentieth century, dozens of Aramean intellectuals and public figures were assassinated in Southeast Turkey, including the former mayor of Beth Zabday (Courtois, 2012). Beth Zabday (Idil) was the only Aramean town that could defend itself at the time of the 1915 genocide, but after the assassination of the former mayor almost all Arameans left Beth Zabday. The son of the murdered former mayor returned from the Diaspora a few years ago, but he was forced to leave Turkey again after his house was blown up (Gusten, 2016, p. 28).

At the beginning of the 21st century, Arameans in Turkey still have to deal with the confiscation of estates and possessions, as in the case of St. Gabriel monastery, where the state even went in appeal on order to go through with the confiscation.

In the case of St. Gabriel Monastery, a group of local residents of the monastery played a negative role by organizing and offering a petition in which the inhabitants of the monastery were spoken of as intruders. In this petition, the predominantly Kurdish signatories demanded that the "illegal occupation" by the bishop residing in St. Gabriel's monastery should be put to an end (Oran, 2011). It is suggested in this petition that the estate of the St. Gabriel monastery is not the property of the monastery, while St. Gabriel monastery was founded in 397 AD and is 900 years older than the Ottoman Empire. Attempts to confiscate St. Gabriel monastery are known, but by no means an isolated incident (World Council of Arameans, 2015, p. 10). For example, the estate of St. Eugene Monastery was occupied by Kurds who are affiliated with the HDP party. Despite mediation efforts by the chairman of the HDP, Selahattin Demirtas, the occupation of the estate was not ended (Haber7.com, 2013). In 2017 alone, the Turkish state expropriated over 100 churches, monasteries, cemeteries, farmlands and other property in Mardin province. After Mardin became a metropolitan municipality (Buyuksehir belediyesi), the villages in the neighborhood of Mardin obtained the status of suburbs. As a result, these villages were tied to the provincial government. Mardin's provincial government has transferred the ownership of more than 100 churches, monasteries, cemeteries, lands and other real estate to the Turkish Ministry of Finance through a special committee (Tasfiye ve Paylastırma Komisyonu). The Turkish Ministry of Finance has subsequently transferred ownership of the churches, monasteries and cemeteries to the Turkish presidency for religious affairs (Diyanet).

The wave of confiscations led to fierce protests from the Aramean community in the diaspora (Ochlast, 2017). In the Netherlands, parliamentary questions were asked about the confiscation of possessions of Arameans in Turkey. The Dutch Minister of Foreign Affairs confirmed that there have been legal proceedings on expropriation of property of Arameans in the province of Mardin, and initiated a field investigation into the confiscation of possessions of Aramean Christians in Turkey (Dutch House of Representatives, 2017). Also at a European level, the expropriation of Aramean property in Turkey was condemned by a motion passed by the European Parliament (European Parliament, 2018). A substantial part of the possessions confiscated in 2017 has since been returned, but the expropriation of Aramean possessions in Turkey remains a structural problem. The 3,000 Arameans still living in south-eastern Turkey (World Council of Arameans, 2015, p. 5) are currently dealing with hundreds of lawsuits related to confiscation of possessions.

Most Arameans currently live in the diaspora, in countries such as Germany, the Netherlands, Sweden, Belgium, Switzerland, Austria, Australia and the United States. In addition, there are Arameans living in Syria, Lebanon, Jordan, Iraq and Israel. Arameans have organized themselves in the diaspora and established national Aramean federations such as the Aramese Federatie in the Netherlands, the Bundesverband der Aramäer in Germany, the Föderation der Aramäer in Switzerland, the Syrianska Riksförbundet in Sweden and the Fedération des Araméens in Belgium.

All these national federations are members of the World Council of Arameans (WCA), the worldwide umbrella organization and the only recognized Aramean NGO with a special consultative status at the United Nations (United Nations). In recent years, the national Aramean federations have lobbied intensively for recognition of the genocide by European countries. In addition, these federations in the diaspora are committed to the rights of oppressed Aramean Christians in Turkey, Syria and Iraq.

Mardin, which means 'fortresses' in Aramaic (Armalet, 1919, p. 1), illustrated by Aydin Atto. In 1915 the homes of Christians in Mardin were marked by means of red crosses (Courtois, 2004, p. 114).

The genocide against Arameans had several dimensions. Besides the elimination of the elite and the mass murders that followed, the confiscation of possessions added an economic dimension to the genocide.

A cultural genocide was committed by changing the names of towns and villages into Turkish names, destroying churches and banning the teaching of the Aramaic language. The Turkification of Aramean regions was a direct assault on the identity of the victims of the genocide. Finally, the denial of the genocide by the Turkish state is an integral part of the genocidal process.

Dimensions of the genocide against Arameans

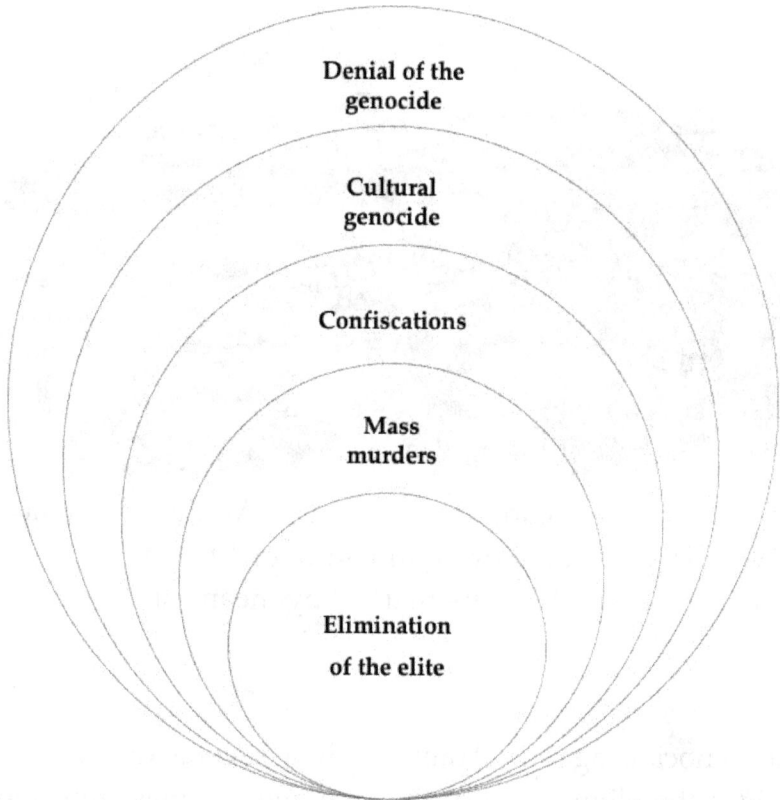

Denial of the
genocide

Cultural
genocide

Confiscations

Mass
murders

Elimination
of the elite

IN MEMORY OF THE MORE
THAN 500,000 ARAMEANS
VICTIMS OF THE
GENOCIDE ORDERED BY THE
OTTOMAN LEADERS OF 1915

A LA MEMOIRE DES PLUS
DE 500.000 VICTIMES
ARAMEENNES DU
GENOCIDE ORDONNE
PAR LES DIRIGEANTS
OTTOMANS DE 1915

TER NAGEDACHTENIS
VAN DE MEER DAN
500.000 ARAMESE
SLACHTOFFERS VAN DE
VOLKENMOORD IN
OPDRACHT VAN
DE OTTOMAANSE
LEIDERS VAN 1915

DRAPEAU DES ARAMEENS - FLAG OF THE ARAMEANS - VLAG VAN DE ARAMEEËRS

The genocide monument in Brussels, in memory of the Aramean victims of the genocide of 1915. With thanks to Luc Atas for the image.

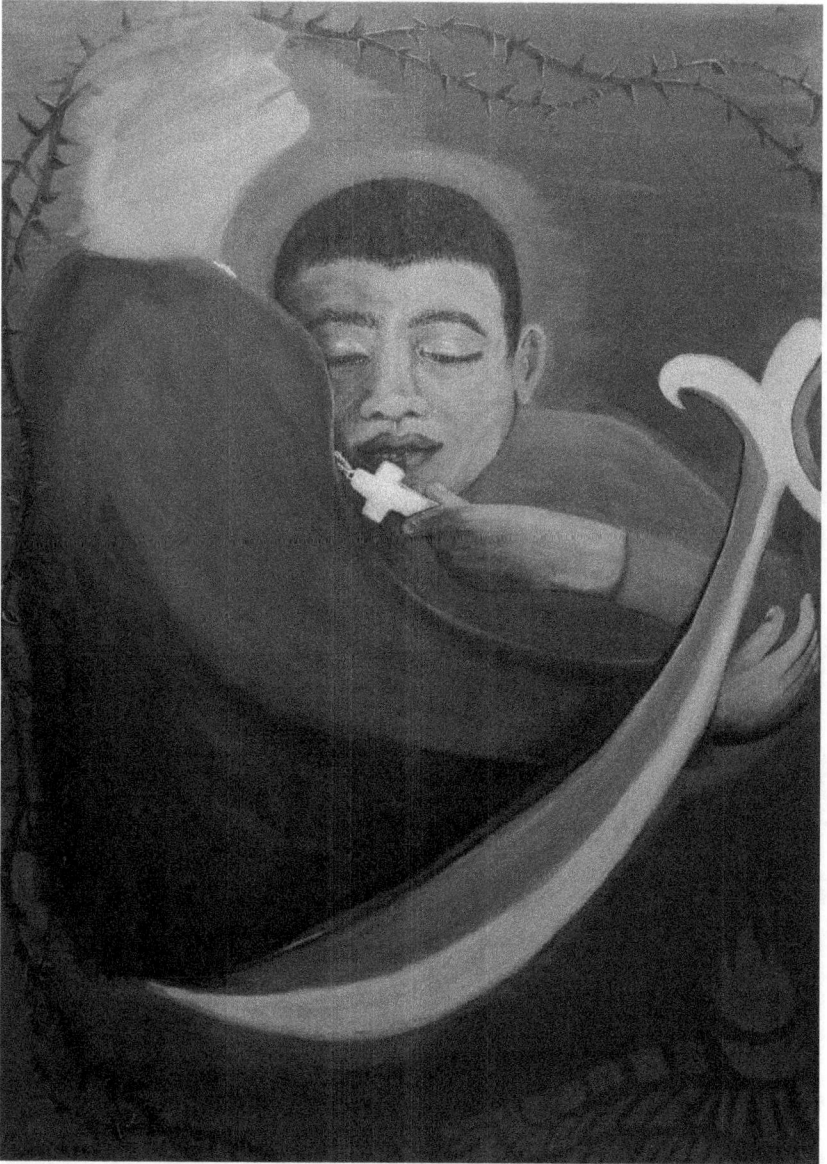

The suffering of children during the genocide of 1915, painted by Aydin Atto.

History repeats itself

The current suffering of Arameans affects me, they are already on the run. This time they are driven away by ISIS and other jihadist groups. History repeats itself for them.

(Can, 2016, p. 143)

A century after the genocide of 1915, Arameans still suffer from the terror of radical groups. Children and grandchildren of genocide survivors are being persecuted by groups such as Islamic State and Al-Nusra. Since the outbreak of the so-called Arab Spring in 2011, Arameans are under enormous pressure in Syria. What started in 2011 with demonstrations, quickly turned into a bloody war. Militant groups fighting against the Syrian army eventually controlled large parts of Syria (Channel 4, 2013). After Homs fell into the hands of rebels and radical groups, almost the entire Christian community of Homs, encompassing some 160 thousand people, including the Aramean community, was forced to flee (U.S. Commission on International Religious Freedom, 2013, p. 11). As the war progressed, the persecution of Arameans increased. On 4 September 2013, the historic Aramean town of Maaloula was occupied by fighters from Al-Nusra. Nuns were kidnapped (Alkhshali, 2013). Fighters from Al-Nusra attacked churches and houses of Arameans. The remaining Arameans were threatened, and in some cases executed if they did not convert to Islam (Daily Mail, 2013, RTL News, 2013, Associated Press, 2013).

Maaloula illustrated by Aydin Atto.

Maaloula is on a UNESCO World Heritage List (UNESCO, 1999) because of its historic churches and because it is one of the oldest centers of Christianity (EO, 2013). After the attack on Maaloula, radical groups wreaked pogroms in historical Aramean towns such as Sadad, which is mentioned in the Bible (Numbers 34:8). In Sadad, 45 Arameans were slaughtered in a gruesome way (Pontifex, 2013). Terrorists committed targeted attacks, such as in Qamishli, where on 30 December 2015 a series of terrorist attacks was committed on Aramean Christians (Van Hoeven ten Voorde, 2016, p. 9). Many priests were murdered or abducted (Ghosh, 2014).

For example, Syriac Orthodox Archbishop Gregorius John Ibrahim and Greek Orthodox Archbishop Paul Yazigi were abducted near Aleppo on April 22, 2013 (World Council of Arameans, 2016, p. 1). Age-old Aramaic heritage was destroyed. In Palmyra, which is called Tadmor by the local inhabitants, the temple of Baal was destroyed by Islamic State (NOS, 2015). Tadmor, which means 'miracle' in Aramaic, was one of the most important archaeological sites in the Middle East. The inhabitants of Palmyra once spoke Palmyrenean, an independently developed form of Aramaic (Klugkist, 1982, p. 11).

Also in Iraq, the "Arab Spring" quickly changed into a civil war. In 2014, Islamic State surprised friend and foe by starting an offensive that resembled the blitzkrieg of Nazi Germany. Within a short period of time, large parts of Iraq and Syria were conquered (Ellian, 2015). In Mosul, houses of Arameans were marked with the Arabic letter N, which stands for Nasrani or Christian. Their possessions were then confiscated. Women were sold by Islamic State as sex slaves (Shea, 2016, pp. 8-11, De Vries, 2016). A woman from Mosul testified how she was abused as a sex slave for two years. Sometimes she was raped by eight different men in one day, after having been forced to marry each rapist and then immediately divorce him (IILHR, MRG, NPWJ, UNPO, 2016, p. 17). Islamic State even published a price list of Christian and Yazidi women (Mamoun, 2014) who were sold as sex slaves (Shea, 2016, p. 3). All churches in areas controlled by Islamic State are destroyed or closed (U.S. Commission on International Religious Freedom, 2016, p. 3).

No millions of innocent people were murdered as they were in 1915, but Islamic State nevertheless committed genocide by systematically cleansing large parts of Syria and Iraq from Arameans, Yazidis and other minorities. The Council of Europe (Omtzigt, 2017, pp. 3 & 9), the European Parliament (European Parliament, 2016) and the US Senate (US Congress - Foreign Affairs | Senate - Foreign Relations, 2016) recognized the genocide that Islamic State has committed against, among others, Christians and Yazidis.

Bibliography

- Alkhshali, H. e. (2013, December 5). Pope: Pray for abducted nuns in Syria. Retrieved from www.cnn.com: http://edition.cnn.com/2013/12/04/world/meast/syria-civil-war/

- Archive.org.(2013, July 16). Retrieved on December 29, 2017, from https://archive.org/details/ChronicleOfMichaelTheGreatPatriarchOfTheSyrians

- Armalet, I. (1919). Al Qusara fi Nakabat an-Nasara - Beirut.

- Armstrong, W. (2016, March 24). The 1909 massacres of Armenians in Adana. Retrieved from www.hurriyetdailynews.com: http://www.hurriyetdailynews.com/opinion/william-armstrong/the-1909-massacres-of-armenians-in-adana-96825

- Associated Press. (2013, September 8). Al Qaeda-linked rebels gain control of Christian village. Retrieved from www.foxnews.com: http://www.foxnews.com/world/2013/09/08/syrian-activists-say-al-qaida-linked-rebels-gain-control-christian-village.html

- Awad, L., & Obeid, M. (2015). Never Forget (Translated by: T. Issa). Damascus: Syrian Orthodox Patriarchate of Antioch and All the East.

- Brock, S. P., & Taylor, D. G. (2001). De verborgen parel: de Syrisch-Orthodoxe kerk en haar oude Aramese erfgoed (Translated by: J. Jonk). Roma: Trans World Film Italia.

- Busstra, H., & Postema , J. (Directors). (2015, April 22). De Vergeten Genocide [Film]. Retrieved from https://www.npo.nl/2doc/22-04-2015/VPWON_1233300

- Can, S. (2016). De Arabische Storm. Amsterdam: Lebowski Publishers.

- Channel 4. (2013, March 27). The jihadist groups 'running the show' in Syria. Retrieved from www.chanel4.com: https://www.channel4.com/news/syria-rebels-jihadist-nusra-war-assad-free-syria-army

- Churchill, W. (1929). The World Crisis, vol. 5, The Aftermath. New York: Charles Scribner's Sons.

- Courtois, S. d. (2004). The Forgotten Genocide: Eastern Christians, The Last Arameans (Translated by: V. Aurora). New Jersey: Gorgias press.

- Courtois, S. d. (2012, May 14). Midyat'ta yeni hayat. Agos. Retrieved from http://www.agos.com.tr/tr/yazi/1380/midyatta-yeni-hayat

- Daily Mail. (2013, September 8). www.dailymail.co.uk. Retrieved from www.dailymail.co.uk: http://www.dailymail.co.uk/news/article-2415586/Syrian-rebels-attack-historic-Christian-village-residents-speak-language-Jesus.html

- D'Avril. (2013). La Chaldee Chretienne, Etude Sur L Histoire Religieuse Et Politique Des Chaldeens Unis. HACHETTE LIVRE-BNF.

- The United Nations. (1948). Retrieved from http://www.un.org/en/genocideprevention/genocide.html

- De Vries, M. (2016, May 27). 'Europa laat christenen in Midden-Oosten in de steek'. Trouw. Retrieved from https://www.trouw.nl/home/-europa-laat-christenen-in-midden-oosten-in-de-steek-~a20d028f/

- Den Biesen, K. (2014). De zingende vrouwen van St. Efrem de Syriër. Glane: Bar Ebroyo Press.

- Ellian, A. (2015, June 5). IS is de zoveelste moordmachine die de politieke islam voortbracht. Elsevier.

- Enver. (1915, November 9). Telegram directed to the leadership of the 3rd Ottoman army - Gunkur, Atase Arsivi, KOL: BDH, KLS: 17, dos. : 81/FIH: 32.

- EO. (2013, September 8). Retrieved from https://www.eo.nl/geloven/nieuws/item/syrische-rebellen-veroveren-christelijk-dorp/

- European parliament. (2016, April 2). MEPs call for urgent action to protect religious minorities against ISIS. Retrieved from www.europarl.europa.eu: http://www.europarl.europa.eu/news/en/news-room/20160129IPR11938/meps-call-for-urgent-action-to-protect-religious-minorities-against-isis

- European parliament. (2018, February 7). www.europarl.europa.eu. Retrieved from http://www.europarl.europa.eu/sides/getDoc.do?pubRef=-//EP//NONSGML+MOTION+B8-2018-0103+0+DOC+PDF+V0//NL

- Gaunt, D. (2006). Massacres, Resistance, Protectors: Muslim-Christian Relations in Eastern Anatolia during World War I. New Jersey: Gorgias Press.

- Ghosh, P. (2014, January 15). Syria's War On Christians: Where Are The Missing Bishops, Priests And Nuns? Retrieved from www.ibtimes.com: http://www.ibtimes.com/syrias-war-christians-where-are-missing-bishops-priests-nuns-1541590

- Gusten, S. (2016). A farewell to Tur Abdin. Istanbul: Istanbul Policy Center.

- Haber7.com. (2013, June 23). www.haber7.com. Retrieved from http://www.haber7.com/guncel/haber/1041793-suryanilerle-bdpliler-arasinda-arazi-kavgasi

- Hain, K. (2012). Devshirme is a Contested Practice. Historia: the Alpha Rho Papers.

- Henno, S. (1977/2005). De vervolging en de uitroeiing van de Syro-Arameeërs in Tur Abdin 1915 (Translated by: J. Jonk). Qahtaniyah, Syrië: Bar Hebraeus Verlag.

- Hofmann, T. (2005). A supplement. In S. Henno, De vervolging en de uitroeiing van de Syro-Arameeërs in Tur Abdin 1915 (Translated by: J. Jonk). Glane: Bar Hebraeus Verlag.

- Holocaust Namenmonument. (2018, April 7). holocaustnamenmonument.nl. Retrieved from https://www.holocaustnamenmonument.nl/nl/holocaust-namenmonument/holocaust-namenmonument-nederland/

- Holslag, A. (2010). In het gesteente van Ararat. Soesterberg: Aspekt.

- IILHR, MRG, NPWJ, UNPO. (2016). No Way Home: Iraq's minorities on the verge of disappearance.

- Iwas, P. I. (1983). Retrieved on April 2, 2018, from syriacstudies.com: http://www.syriacstudies.com/2017/09/19/the-syrian-orthodox-church-of-antioch-at-a-glance-patriarch-ignatius-zakka-i-iwas-1983-translated-by-emmanuel-h-bismarji/

- Jansen, H. (2008). Islam voor varkens, apen, ezels en andere beesten. Amsterdam: Uitgeverij Van Praag.

- Jenkins, P. (2011). Het vergeten christendom (Translated by: H. Moerdijk). Amsterdam: Nieuw Amsterdam Uitgevers.

- Kevorkian, R. (2011). The Armenian Genocide: A Complete History. New York: I.B.Tauris & Co Ltd.

- Klugkist, A. C. (1982, April 17). Midden-Aramese schriften in Syrië, Mesopotamië, Perzië en aangrenzende gebieden. University of Groningen.

- Leijsen, L. v. (2015, November 23). www.oecumene.nl. Retrieved from http://www.oecumene.nl/documentatie/christenen-in-het-midden-oosten/1098-christenen-van-syrie-een-inleiding

- Lepsius, J. (1919). Der Todesgang des Armenischen Volkes Bericht über das Schicksal des Armenischen Volkes in der Türkei während des Weltkrieges. Potsdam, Duitsland: Der Tempelverlag.

- Luke, I. C. (1925). Mosul and Its Minorities. London. Retrieved from www.syriacstudies.com: http://www.syriacstudies.com/AFSS/Syriac_Articles_in_English/Entries/2007/10/12_The_SYRIANS_IN_TUR_ABDIN_-_DR._JOHN_JOSEPH.html

- MacLeod, E. (2015, May 27). Jesus Spoke Aramaic: The Reasons Why, And Why It Matters. Createspace Independent Publishing Platform.

- Mamoun, A. (2014, November 3). www.iraqinews.com. Retrieved from www.iraqinews.com: http://cdn.iraqinews.com/wp-content/uploads/2014/11/ggt.jpg

- Masters, B. (1990). THE 1850 EVENTS IN ALEPPO. International Journal of Middle East Studies, Vol. 22, No. 1, 3-20.

- Messo, J. (2011). De christelijke Arameeërs onder het juk van de islam. In S. van Rooy, & W. van Rooy, De Islam: kritische essays over een politieke religie. Aspekt.

- Messo, J. (2017). Arameans and the making of Assyrians. Aramaic Press.

- NOS. (2015, September 1). Tempel van Bel is wel vernield. Retrieved from www.nos.nl: http://nos.nl/artikel/2055279-vn-tempel-van-bel-is-wel-vernield.html

- O-bible.com. Retrieved on January 1, 2018, from o-bible.com: http://www.o-bible.com/BiblicalInformation/index.html#!ANOINTED-PEOPLE-PEOPLE-WHO-WERE-ANOINTED-PHYSICALLY

- Ochlast, S. (2017, June 28). www.domradio.de. Retrieved from https://www.domradio.de/themen/kirche-und-politik/2017-06-28/konrad-adenauer-stiftung-zu-kirchenenteignungen-der-tuerkei

- Oktem, K. (2004). Incorporating the time and space of the ethnic other: nationalism and space in Southeast Turkey in the nineteenth and twentieth centuries. Nations and Nationalism(10 (4)).

- Omtzigt, P. (2017, September 22). Parliamentary Assembly of the Council of Europe. Retrieved from http://assembly.coe.int: http://semantic-pace.net/tools/pdf.aspx?doc=aHR0cDovL2Fzc2VtYmx5Lm NvZS5pbnQvbncveG1sL1hSZWYvWDJILURXLWV4dHIu YXNwP2ZpbGVpZD0yNDAxNCZsYW5nPUVO&xsl=aHR 0cDovL3NlbWFudGljcGFjZS5uZXQvWHNsdC9QZGYvW FJlZi1XRC1BVC1YTUwyUERGLnhzbA==&xsltparams=Zm lsZWlkPTI0MDE0

- Oran, B. (2011, February 17). Retrieved on March 10, 2018, from http://www.suryoyo.uni-goettingen.de/news/morgabriel-Baskinoran.html

- Pontifex, J. (2013, November 5). Syria: Death and Destruction in Christian town of Sadad. Retrieved from www.acnuk.org: http://www.acnuk.org/news.php/455/syria-death-and-destruction-in-christian-town-of-sadad

- RTL Nieuws. (2013, September 15). 'Drie kogels in zijn hoofd omdat hij christen was'. (R. Konijnebelt, Redacteur, & RTL) Retrieved on May 25, 2017, from youtube: https://youtu.be/TKb1ti3NHrI

- Shea, N. (2016). The ISIS Genocide of Middle Eastern Christian Minorities. Washington, D.C.: Hudson Institute.

- Shwartz, E. Y. (2005). My Life's Story. Jeruzalem: Alon Printing.

- Sommer, B. (2018, March 1). Turkije neemt Nederland de maat over slavernijverleden. Elsevier Weekblad.

- Sommer, R. (2012). Religious Freedom in the Context of the Accession Negotiations between the European Union and Turkey - The Example of the Arameans. M. T. Pieter Omtzigt, The slow disappearance of the Syriacs from Turkey and of the Grounds of the Mor Gabriel Monastery (p. 163). Lit verlag.

- The New York Times. (1860, August 20). The Damascus Massacres. Retrieved on April 2, 2018, from https://www.nytimes.com/1860/08/20/archives/the-damascus-massacres-letter-from-abdelkader.html

- Treaty of Lausanne - Art: 40. (1923, Juli 24). Retrieved on April 12, 2018, from wwi.lib.byu.edu: https://wwi.lib.byu.edu/index.php/Treaty_of_Lausanne

- Tweede Kamer. (2018, February 22). Retrieved from www.tweedekamer.nl: https://www.tweedekamer.nl/downloads/document?id=0e190c6e-1a87-47de-b7aa-9d0c68604e47&title=Motie%20van%20het%20lid%20Voordewind%20c.s.%20over%20erkennen%20van%20de%20Armeense%20genocide.pdf

- U.S. Commission on International Religious Freedom. (2013). Protecting and Promoting Religious Freedom in Syria. Washington: U.S. Commission on International Religious Freedom.

- U.S. Commission on International Religious Freedom. (2016). Retrieved from http://www.uscirf.gov/sites/default/files/USCIRF_AR_2016_Tier1_2_Syria.pdf

- U.S. Congress - Foreign Affairs | Senate - Foreign Relations. (2016, March15). H.Con.Res.75 - Expressing the sense of Congress that the atrocities perpetrated by ISIL against religious and ethnic minorities in Iraq and Syria include war crimes, crimes against humanity, and genocide. Retrieved from www.congress.gov: https://www.congress.gov/bill/114th-congress/house-concurrent-resolution/75

- UNESCO. (1999). Maaloula. Retrieved from van whc.unesco.org: http://whc.unesco.org/en/tentativelists/1299/

- Ungor, U. (2009, Maart 25). (V. d. Résistance, Producent) Retrieved from http://www.sciencespo.fr/mass-violence-war-massacre-resistance/fr/document/diyarbekir-1915-1916-young-turk-mass-killings-provincial-level

- Ungor, U. (2012). De Armeense genocide. T. Zwaan, U. U. Ungor, M. Mennecke, B. Kiernan, W. t. Have, & M. v. Haperen, De Holocaust en andere genociden . Amsterdam: Amsterdam University Press. Retrieved on January 7, 2018, from www.niod.nl: https://www.niod.nl/sites/niod.nl/files/Armeense%20genoc ide.pdf

- Ungor, U. (2013, October 13). Retrieved on January 26, 2018, from www.gagrule.net: https://gagrule.net/turkish-prof-ugur-ungor-discusses-armenian-genocide-western-armenia-became-part-turkish-state-confiscation-destruction-armenian-properteis-video/

- Ungor, U. (2017). HOW ARMENIAN WAS THE 1915 GENOCIDE? Let Them Not Return. New York: Berghahn Books.

- United Nations. www.esango.un.org. Retrieved on April 12, 2018, from http://esango.un.org/civilsociety/simpleSearch.do?method= search&searchTypeRedef=simpleSearch&sessionCheck=fal se&searchType=simpleSearch&organizationNamee=world +council+of+arameans

- Van Hoeven ten Voorde, J. (2016, January 7). Syrische christenen leven in angst. Reformatorisch Dagblad, p. 9.

- Van Qarabash, A. M. (1918/2002). Vergoten Bloed (Translated by: J. Jonk). Mardin: Bar Hebraeus Verlag.

- World Council of Arameans. (2015, March 16). The Aramean (Syriac) Christians of Turkey: The Case of a Forgotten People. Retrieved from www.aramesefederatie.org: https://aramesefederatie.files.wordpress.com/2017/07/the-aramean-christians-of-turkey.pdf

- World Council of Arameans. (2016, April 22). www.wca-ngo.org. Retrieved from http://www.wca-ngo.org/images/PDF/documents/WCA_Report_Neglected_ Bishops_220416.pdf

- Zürcher, E.-J. (2016). The Ottoman Jihad, the German Jihad and the Sacralization of War. 20.

- Zwaan, T. (2001). Civilisering En Decivilisering. Amsterdam: Boom.

- Zwaan, T. (2004). De vergeten genocide. Auschwitz Bulletin, pp. Jaargang 5, no. 17.

Recognition of the genocide by the Dutch House of Representatives

Tweede Kamer der Staten-Generaal

2

Vergaderjaar 2017–2018

34 775 V	Vaststelling van de begrotingsstaat van het Ministerie van Buitenlandse Zaken (V) voor het jaar 2018

Nr. 56	**MOTIE VAN HET LID VOORDEWIND C.S.** Voorgesteld 22 februari 2018

De Kamer,

gehoord de beraadslaging,

overwegende dat het advies van de CAVV en de EVA (Externe Volkenrechtelijke Adviseur) constateert dat regering en parlement een genocide kunnen erkennen en dat dit ook betekenis is;

spreekt uit dat de Kamer de Armeense genocide erkent (voor de volledigheid gaat het hier ook over de Assyriërs, de Pontische Grieken en Arameeërs die eveneens het slachtoffer zijn geworden van deze genocide),

en gaat over tot de orde van de dag.

Voordewind
Ten Broeke
Van Helvert
Sjoerdsma
Van Ojik
Karabulut
Van Raan
Krol
Van der Staaij
Baudet

kst 34775 V-56
ISSN 0921 - 7371
's Gravenhage 2018

Source: (Tweede Kamer, 2018)